Further praise for *Felon*

"Searing. . . . This is a powerful work of lyric art. It is also a tour de force indictment of the carceral industrial state."

—Carolyn Forché, *New York Times Book Review*

"[Reginald Dwayne] Betts is a hero to men on the inside. . . . He's a hero to anyone who believes redemption can be had and is not some abstract idea. *Felon* is a testament to Betts's talent and success, but when you read it deeply and feel it and celebrate its ideas, the layers peel back. I imagine it will leave you not only informed, but saddened, as it did me."

—John J. Lennon, *Poetry Foundation*

"[A] lyric account of the butterfly effects of incarceration. . . . *Felon* is a magnum opus of what it means to live in American society. . . . This sort of collection enumerates the best that poetry can be: a tool, a song, a gesture towards empathy, an enactment of living a life that continues to baffle."

—Kassy Lee, *Michigan Quarterly Review*

"Whether delivering a one-two punch reminiscent of rap or the quiet revelations of a man brimming with wisdom, the poems in Reginald Dwayne Betts' *Felon* traverse the realities of re-entering society post-incarceration."

—Lauren LaRocca, *Baltimore* magazine

"In visually arresting poems, Betts exposes systematic prejudices, legal disparities, and the emotional strain of raising two sons in a country accustomed to assuming the worst about Black males. . . . The importance of Betts' collection cannot be overstated as current events shed light on ongoing injustices." —*Booklist*

"On every page of *Felon*, a book unlike anything I've ever experienced, there's something far more playful, resonant, and ruggedly revealing happening. Reginald Dwayne Betts animates and really embodies the minutiae of revision in this once-in-a-lifetime art object. . . . Betts's artistry shows and proves a necessary breaking and blurring of the lines between wandering into yesterday, wondering into tomorrow, and wrestling with the funk of today. Betts has written the twenty-first-century book that will dictate how freedom, power, and consequence are written about until the sun says enough. It is that good."

—Kiese Laymon, author of *Heavy: An American Memoir*

"*Felon* is the keenest of testaments to what it's like to have lived behind the walls, to the crucible of having one's humanity challenged, changed, erased, to how—for the anointed—prisons persist beyond the walls. While there are poems aplenty on the mental and physical violence of prison and our unjustice system, the collection is also a moving exploration of love—romantic and familial—and how one nurtures that love against odds that at times seem impossible. *Felon* is bracing, revelatory work. Read it and be transformed."   —Mitchell S. Jackson, author of *Survival Math*

"*Felon* is a stunningly crafted indictment of prison's dehumanization of Black men and their loved ones. Through his unvarnished descriptions of the path to prison and its aftermath from myriad vantage points—son, husband, father, cellmate, Yale-educated public defender—Betts does nothing to protect himself, or us, from what he has done and suffered and witnessed. His compassion and breathtaking literary gifts make it impossible for us to look away or remain complicit in mass criminalization's status quo."

—sujatha baliga, director of the Restorative Justice Project

FELON

W. W. NORTON & COMPANY

Independent Publishers Since 1923

FELON

POEMS

REGINALD DWAYNE BETTS

Cover art by Titus Kaphar, excerpt from a body of work entitled The Jerome Project.
kapharstudio.com

For information about permission to reproduce selections from this book, write to
Permissions, W. W. Norton & Company, Inc., 500 Fifth Avenue, New York, NY 10110

For information about special discounts for bulk purchases, please contact
W. W. Norton Special Sales at specialsales@wwnorton.com or 800-233-4830

Manufacturing by Versa Press
Book design by JAM Design
Production manager: Beth Steidle

Library of Congress Cataloging-in-Publication Data

Names: Betts, Reginald Dwayne, 1980– author.
Title: Felon : poems / Reginald Dwayne Betts.
Description: First edition. | New York, NY : W. W. Norton & Company, Inc., [2019]
Identifiers: LCCN 2019026008 | ISBN 9780393652147 (hardcover) | ISBN 9780393652154 (epub)
Classification: LCC PS3602.E826 A6 2019 | DDC 811/.6—dc23
LC record available at https://lccn.loc.gov/2019026008

ISBN 978-0-393-54203-5 pbk.

W. W. Norton & Company, Inc., 500 Fifth Avenue, New York, N.Y. 10110
www.wwnorton.com

W. W. Norton & Company Ltd., 15 Carlisle Street, London W1D 3BS

3 4 5 6 7 8 9 0

To Terese, Micah, and Miles:

for love; for the many moments I cherish, and every regret; for all of it.

CONTENTS

FELON

GHAZAL

Name a song that tells a man what to expect after prison;
Explains Occam's razor: you're still a suspect after prison.

Titus Kaphar painted my portrait, then dipped it in black tar.
He knows redaction is a dialect after prison.

From inside a cell, the night sky isn't the measure—
that's why it's prison's vastness your eyes reflect after prison.

My lover don't believe in my sadness. She says whisky,
not time, is what left me wrecked after prison.

Ruth, Papermaker, take these tattered gray sweats.
Make paper of my bid: a past I won't reject after prison.

The state murdered Kalief with a single high bail.
Always innocent. Did he fear time's effect after prison?

Dear Warden, my time been served, let me go,
Promise that some of this I won't recollect—after prison.

My mother has died. My father, a brother & two cousins.
There is no G-d; no reason to genuflect, after prison.

Jeremy & Forest rejected the template, said for
it to be funky, the font must redact after prison.

.   .   .

He came home saying righteous, coochie, & jive turkey.
All them lost years, his slang's architect after prison.

The Printer silkscreens a world onto black paper.
With ink, Erik reveals what we neglect after prison.

My homeboy say he's done with all that prison shit.
His wife & baby girl gave him love to protect after prison.

Them fools say you can become anything when it's over.
Told 'em straight up, ain't nothing to resurrect after prison.

You have come so far, Beloved, & for what, another song?
Then sing. Shahid you're loved, not shipwrecked, after prison.

BLOOD HISTORY

The things that abandon you get remembered different.
As precise as the English language can be, with words
like *penultimate* & *perseverate*, there is not a combination
of sounds that describe only that leaving. Once,
drinking & smoking with buddies, a friend asked if
I'd longed for a father. Had he said wanted, I would have
dismissed him in the way that youngins dismiss it all:
a shrug, sarcasm, a jab to his stomach, laughter.
But he said longing. & in a different place, I might
have wept. Said, once, my father lived with us & then he
didn't & it fucked me up so much I never thought about
his leaving until I held my own son in my arms & only
now speak on it. A man who drank Boone's Farm & Mad
Dog like water once told me & some friends that there is no
word for father where he comes from, not like we know it.
There, the word father is the same as the word for listen.
The blunts we passed around let us forget our
tongues. Not that much though. But what if the old
head knew something? & if you have no father, you can't
hear straight. Years later, another friend wondered why
I named my son after my father. *You know, that's a thing*
turn your life to a prayer that no dead man gonna answer.

THE LORD MIGHT HAVE GIVEN HIM WINGS

There was something
      wrong with him,
our poor thing.

& if prison is where Black

     men go to become
Lazarus (or to become Jonah),
      this kid must

already have wings.

They call it inevitable,

everything
      after that hour's confession:

The silences & walls that drown
             the living.
(& what of his victims,

their skin as dark as the night?)
      No one calls him

kid. The arms
     he slides in a sweater (for
protection against

. . .

the cold) slender enough
                    to fit in the fist
of a large man

            is what I mean. (His hands
large enough to grip the black
            of the pistol, to squeeze the quiver

of a trigger.) The holy
            have left, we know.

& the kid, his halo
a mess of hurt (the daffodils of poverty,

            & the ones who abandoned him),

his sentence a cataclysm
            of the guns he pulled
& the dirt shrouded dead

teenagers in cities he's
            never known. When they name mass

incarceration, he will be
amongst
            the number, & the victim's mother,
her Black invisible against

the subtext of her son's coffin,
                    will be on the outside
            of advocacy. The kid

. . .

has folded his wings
        into his body & though he needs
flight, now, there are only

        years to fulfill
his need for escape. Shorn
        now & the corridors

before him are as long
        as the Atlantic, each cell
a wave threatening

to coffle him. No
        one believed he'd
make such a beautiful corpse.

BEHIND YELLOW TAPE

Half what they say about what they'll do
with the ratchet is a lie. The weight of death,
worn so near a man's crotch, can't help
but fuck with them. But who among us
had a holster? Had been before a firing squad?
None of us laughed when Burress shot himself,
we knew a few who blew small holes in clothes,
feet, sheetrock, while reckless with a burner
off safety. That danger & prison should have
made us pause. But, statistics ain't prophecy,
& ain't none of us expect to be in the NFL
or a cell. The truth somewhere between.
Like when me, Thomas, & Sam's brother
all beat the shit out of that boy with the lopsided
edge-up. At first, it was a fair fight, & for real,
Thomas just wanted to break it up. But the boy
struck back & it became fuck it. Intervention
turned intervening. Or like how I felt Slim ain't
deserve the grave no more than his killer earned
those 78 years. But that don't make the prison
they turned into the killer's tomb slavery.
We all standing on the wrong side of choices.
When we stomped & stomped & pummeled
that boy, we carried massacre in our eyes.
Half of all of this is about regret. A cage never
followed my smacking the woman that I love. But
for kicking a mud hole in that kid we'd become
felons. All the stories I keep to myself tell how

violence broke & made me, turned me into a man
can't forget the face of a young boy bleeding out
as if his blood would make the scorched asphalt
grow something loved, & beautiful.

LOSING HER

When I was sweating & telling that woman
my bad, sorry, please don't go. I'd drunk
a world of whisky. I couldn't sing if I wanted.
G-d was throwing dice against my skull. I had lied
to her for more days than Jesus spent in the wilderness.
They say he was in the desert but I know
the wilderness is worst. Ain't no mirages in the wild,
& with whisky flowing like gospel in my veins,
I could hear her sit a shotgun by the door I once
carried her through singing *Real Love*. Before I
started banging on the door, I called her house phone,
dialed numbers from a decade before things
went digital. I been loving her so long. But she ain't
answer. That number from back when our love
was three-way phone calls & laughter & hands
that didn't treat her body like a threat. Back then,
she loved me in a way she don't now & so I banged
on that door as if I was the police & I started weeping
& my body slumped—trying, but failing, to call her name.

WHISKY FOR BREAKFAST

My liver, awash in all but dregs
                    of a charred oak cask,
        soaked in barley's amber,
                    shadowed as blood, dim
as a cell in the hole, survived
                    brackish prison water
        only to become collateral. The things
                    that haunt me still,

drown, now, friends say, in nearly
                    fifty pounds of brick-
        hued rotgut. Spiritus frumenti.
A gallon of whisky
        weighs eight pounds. & all this
                    becomes a man confessing
that he's riven. & I drink.

                    Mornings I turn sunrise into
another empty glass & a
                    dozen angels diving
behind the mire I swallow to
                    save my body from itself.
                    All scream,

me &, even, the cherubim, lost
        in that smoky, dense
comfort, lost in darkness & sometimes,
        I swear,
                    even G-d has no alibi.

FOR A BAIL DENIED

for A.S.

I won't tell you how it ended, &
his mother won't, either, but beside
me she stood & some things neither

of us could know, & now, all is lost;
lost is all in what came after—the kid,
& we should call him kid, call him a

child, his face smooth & without history
of a razor, he shuffled—ghostly—into
court, & let's just call it a cauldron, &

admit his nappy head made him blacker
than whatever pistol he'd held,
whatever solitary awaited; the prosecutor's

bald head was black or brown (but
when has brown not been akin to Black
here? to abyss?) & does it matter,

Black lives, when all he said of Black
boys was that they kill?—the child beside
his mother & his mother beside me &

I am not his father, just a public
defender, near starving, here, where the
state turns men, women, children into

.   .   .

numbers, seeking something more useful
than a guilty plea & this boy beside
me's withering, on the brink of life &

broken, & it's all possible, because the
judge spoke & the kid says
—*I did it I mean I did it I mean Jesus*—

someone wailed & the boy's mother yells:
*This ain't justice. You can't throw my son
into that fucking ocean.* She meant jail.

& we was powerless to stop it.
& too damn tired to be beautiful.

TRIPTYCH

But for is always game.
A man can be murdered
twice, but for science;
his body a pool of blood
in Baltimore & Tulsa,
except, it isn't, his body actually
slender against the sunlight just
outside a California prison. A crow
rests on a fence near his car.
Visiting hours long done
(for man not crow,
one of a murderous many
that flies above this barbed wire),
& the cigarette he smokes
is illegal, here, & but for
the magnetic pull tragedy
has on Black women, he wouldn't be
here, right now, contemplating
the crimson colored man leaping
into the darkness on his J's.
He still says Air Jordans,
because air is important,
swearing to Black America's
aim, if not ability, to soar,
a way to outrun statistics
& the lead in the water.
Alas, metaphysics says
you are only you & no one

else, & a Black poet says Black
love is not one or one thousand
things, & it all may be true,
but for the fact that the man swears
the crow looks at him dead
as if he is already so,
as if while standing there he
has been murdered
by his brother, murdered
by a cop, & bodied
by a prison sentence as flames
from a Newport's burning ash
fail to illuminate his shadow.

WHEN I THINK OF TAMIR RICE WHILE DRIVING

in the backseat my sons laugh & tussle,
far from Tamir's age, adorned with his
complexion & cadence & already warned

about toy pistols, though my rhetoric
ain't about fear, but dislike—about
how guns have haunted me since I first gripped

a pistol; I think of Tamir, twice-blink
& confront my weeping's inadequacy, how
some loss invents the geometry that baffles.

The Second Amendment—cold, cruel,
a constitutional violence, a ruthless
thing worrying me still; should be it predicts

the heft in my hand, arm sag, burdened by
what I bear: My bare arms collaged
with wings as if hope alone can bring

back a buried child. A child, a toy gun,
a blue shield's rapid rapid rabid shit. This
is how misery sounds: my boys

playing in the backseat juxtaposed against
a twelve-year-old's murder playing
in my head. My tongue cleaves to the roof

. . .

of my mouth, my right hand has forgotten.
This is the brick & mortar of the America
that murdered Tamir & may stalk the laughter

in my backseat. I am a father driving
his Black sons to school & the death
of a Black boy rides shotgun & this

could be a funeral procession. The death
a silent thing in the air, unmentioned—
because mentioning death invites taboo:

if you touch my sons the blood washed
away from the concrete must, at some
point, belong to you, & not just to you, to

the artifice of justice that is draped like a blue
g-d around your shoulders, the badge that
justifies the echo of the fired pistol; taboo:

the thing that says freedom is a murderer's body
mangled & disrupted by my constitutional
rights come to burden, because the killer's mind

refused the narrative of a brown child, his dignity,
his right to breathe, his actual fucking existence,
with all the crystalline brilliance I saw when

my boys first reached for me. This world best
invite more than the story of the children bleeding
on crisp fall days. Tamir's death must be more

. . .

than warning about recklessness & abandoned
justice & white terror's ghost—& this is
why I hate it all, the protests & their counters,

the Civil Rights attorneys that stalk the bodies
of the murdered, this dance of ours that reduces
humanity to the dichotomy of the veil. We are

not permitted to articulate the reasons we might
yearn to see a man die. A mind may abandon
sanity. What if all I had stomach for was blood?

But history is no sieve & sanity is no elixir
& I am bound to be haunted by the strength
that lets Tamir's father, mother, kinfolk resist

the temptation to turn everything they see
into a grave & make home the series of cells
that so many brothers already call their tomb.

IN ALABAMA

IN THE ▮▮▮▮▮ MIDDLE ▮▮▮ OF ALABAMA

v

THE CITY OF MONTGOMERY

The Plaintiffs ▮▮▮ ▮▮ impoverished ▮▮▮ jailed by the City ▮▮▮▮ unable to pay ▮▮▮ traffic tickets ▮▮▮▮ pay ▮▮ or ▮ sit ▮▮▮ in ▮▮ jail ▮▮ $50 per day ▮▮ Plaintiffs ▮▮▮ unable to pay ▮▮ each ▮ sent to jail ▮▮▮▮ ▮▮▮▮▮ told ▮ they could ▮▮▮ work ▮ off ▮ debts ▮▮ $25 per day ▮▮ ▮▮ cleaning the ▮▮ City ▮▮ scrubbing feces and blood from jail floors ▮▮▮

18

The treatment ██████████████████████████████

██████████ reveals ███████████████ the

City ███████ against ████ its poorest ██████████████

██

████████████ jailing people if they ████ poor ██████

████████████████████████████████ ████

███

████████ Plaintiffs seek ████████████████████

fundamental rights ████████████ they suffered ████████

████████████████████████████████ the

City s ████████ unlawful ██████████ ████████████████

████ ██████████████████████████████████

██████████████████████████████████████

██████████████████████████████████████

19

It is the policy   of the City   to jail people

It is the policy   of the City to jail   people

It is the policy   of the City to hold prisoners

until   extinguished

It is the policy

It is

the policy

Plaintiffs seek   relief

a 23-year-old woman   mother of two

police officers came

arrested her   she owed the City

Officers took   away   her two children

she   too poor to pay

told   she would   serve

taken   to   jail

Desperate to get back   children

labored to clean

jail bars

a 58-year-old disabled   resident

arrested

took   into custody

kept   for three days

informed   he would

be released   if   someone   pay

asked   for mercy

The court

ordered him to serve 44

days

38-year-old father ▮ lives ▮
▮ with ▮ his children ▮
▮ went to ▮ police ▮ after he
learned ▮ he had ▮ warrants ▮ ▮ traffic tickets ▮
▮ arrested ▮ placed in ▮ jail ▮
▮ kept overnight ▮
▮ he owed
the City ▮ $1,600 ▮ ▮
▮ The judge ▮
ordered him jailed ▮
▮ told ▮
▮ released if he ▮ served 23 days ▮
▮ told ▮ he could work off his
debt ▮
▮
▮ ▮
▮ did not want to clean ▮
▮ blood and feces ▮ desperate ▮
▮ agreed to clean ▮ blood and feces from the jail floors ▮
▮ lost his job while he sat in ▮ jail ▮

Montgomery Violated

Plaintiffs rights by jailing them by
threatening to jail them

Defendant s policy

violates the

Constitution City Violated

The City s policy

violates

Constitution

<u>Request for</u>
<u>Relief</u>

WHEREFORE Plaintiffs request ███████████████ relief

equal protection

judgment

constitutional and

statutory rights

equal protection

judgment

Fourth and

Fourteenth Amendment rights

A ████ judgment ████████ due process ██ equal
protection ████████ rights

Respectfully submitted

A MAN DROPS A COAT ON THE SIDEWALK & ALMOST FALLS INTO THE ARMS OF ANOTHER

for N.D.

as in almost Madame Cezanne in Red,
almost falling, almost no longer—as in
almost only bent elbows, almost more
than longing, almost more than unholy,
more than skag, white lady, junk, almost

more than the city eclipsing around them . . .
Winchester Gun Factory's windows as broken
as the pair refuse to be, the two of them
nodding off of diesel, almost greater
than everything missing, the brown sugar,
the adrenaline slowing them down,
the remnants of a civilization emptied
into their veins. The falling man grasps
at the air. Lost in a trance.

These two, anchored by a coat that nearly
slips from a nameless man's fingers
as he leans parallel to the concrete,
as his arms reach for something absent.
Whatever about reaping. The men eclipse
the sidewalk, & everything else around
them & they sway with a funeral's pace.
These two, their bodies a still-life lover's

.   .   .

drag. I'm in the car with Nicky & we cannot
stop watching. I imagine one whispers *I wish
I never touched it.* But who, in the middle
of a high that lets you escape time utters
such bullshit. One lacks sleeves; the other
throws seven punches into the air
like an aging featherweight. I learned to box

desiring not to be broken or haunted by
my dreams. & when Boxer throws six
jabs at a cushion of air, I know once
they both wanted to be something more
than whatever we watching imagine.

A car stops in the street. No hazards.
Just stops. & a photographing arm extends
the camera offering history as the only help
the two will get: a mechanical witness.
I photo them capturing this world slowed
to loss, the two men now someone's memory.
One almost caresses the face of the other.
Lovers are never this gentle, are never this

close to falling & never patient enough to know
that there is no getting up from some depths.
A perfect day that's just like doom. Own so
fucking world. They lean into each other
without touching. Horse has slowed down
everything. High like that, you can walk for

.   .   .

hours, & imagine, always that there is a needle
waiting for your veins. & Nicky says it's a wonder
how something that can have you hold another so
gently could be the ruin of all you might touch.

CITY OF THE MOON

for JB

There walks a man, somewhere,
Wanting the touch of another
Man & somewhere people know
That desire; name the walking man after
You—Jericho, because G-d once
Promised to bring a city to its knees
For the man circling you with
His trumpet. Going down from
Jerusalem a man broke another
Man, they say, those men lost in
Gospel & what G-d can't fathom:
Odalisque & outstretched arm. They
Don't know every love is a kind
Of robbery. & sometimes hurt
Is a kind of mending. A body only
Broken by death. Every moan ain't
A cry. This is always about vulnerability.
How others afraid to touch a man
Who touches a man have need to
Imagine hips & the flesh they flank
As a confession: the body threatens.
Call that fear suffering. The heathen
Is always afraid of a warm body
Against his own. & while some say
Things always return to a man
& his desire to be touched, & touch,
That want to be known, governs us all.

DIESEL THERAPY

His mother told him. Airport bars always pour something nice. Distance makes bartenders understand suffering. That Thursday he was headed fourteen cities away from anyone he knew & the brown was fortification. His daddy built houses. Those that grown men create in their mind & lock themselves inside. The doctors called it bipolar but his moms just said his pops had some shit with him. Turned his head into an airport. He was always running away from something, always fourteen cities away from the people that loved him, even if they were in the house with him. Everything reminded his father of the feds. He'll say his father taught him to crave brown liquor. Lighter fluid for the brain he would say, as if he, the father, thought it would drown out the noise. Half a dozen years out of prison & every time he walks into an airport he thinks about his father. When he stares down a nice long taste of whisky, he almost wishes there were voices in his head he wanted to drown out—wishes the distance he traveled was something with him, & not the way he stole away from things he couldn't handle.

IF ABSENCE WAS THE SOURCE OF SILENCE

some things my sons would never hear,
not from my reluctance to speak,
or the thief that has silenced his mother's
tongue, his grandmother's tongue,
turned the stare of the woman who, when
it's far too early for the sun to be out,
sees me turn a corner with a Newport,
the sky & the ground as dark as the fear
& yesterdays she swallows as she crosses
into what might as well be oncoming traffic,
remembering a man from her past—
stories my sons would not know,
not because of a need to hide history,
those bedrooms & boardrooms & work
where trust became carnage;
no, these things would be Pandora's box
untouched. & yet, they will know—because.
& the because is what I tell my sons,
about what their hands might do, in long
conversations about what the hands
of men do. Their hands, my own.
When I was twelve, a friend
told me of men offering her money
for her slender & young body, she
no older than me then, arms not strong
enough to carry her own weight, let alone
push her past the men who wanted
to own what is hers. Hers just the first

of a story that would keep returning.
The numbered hurt. Rape, its aftermath
& this account of trauma my boys
would never know if the world differed,
if war did not mean soldiers demanding
the body of a woman as land to plunder.
I keep trying to turn this into sense.
From me, my sons will hear a story about
how hands like theirs, like mine, made
something wretched of the memories
of women we love or don't know at all. This
is true. & there is a map to take us to
all that hurt. Some silence saying it all. But
let's say the world is ours. On that day
all the silenced tongues would have
speak, without fear of being doubted,
of the cars & hellos that became dungeons,
of friends who became the darkness
that drowns all until only rage & sadness
remain. & maybe after, we can build
memory that does not demand silence;
all the things that happen now, as if
a part of being, would not be—
& my sons' lives would be carved
out of days in which their hands
& bodies do not suggest weapons,
days where all their mothers
& sisters can walk down any street
in this world with the freedom
that comes from knowing
you will be safe, after dusk or during

those moments just before dawn
unlike today, & yesterday, & now,
when, the quiet & what might ruin
it, is the threat that circles.

ESSAY ON REENTRY

At two a.m., without enough spirits
spilling into my liver to know
to keep my mouth shut, my youngest
learned of years I spent inside a box: a spell,
a kind of incantation I was under; not whisky,
but History: I robbed a man. This, months
before he would drop bucket after bucket
on opposing players, the entire bedraggled
bunch five & six & he leaping as if
every lay-up erases something. That's how
I saw it, my screaming-coaching-sweating
presence recompense for the pen. My father
has never seen me play ball is part of this.
My oldest knew, told of my crimes by
a stranger. Tell me we aren't running
towards failure is what I want to ask my sons,
but it is two in the a.m. The oldest has gone off
to dream in the comfort of his room, the youngest
despite him seeming more lucid than me,
just reflects cartoons back from his eyes.
So when he tells me, Daddy it's okay, I know
what's happening is some straggling angel,
lost from his pack finding a way to fulfill his
duty, lending words to this kid who crawls
into my arms, wanting, more than stories
of my prison, the sleep that he fought while
I held court at a bar with men who knew

that when the drinking was done,
the drinking wouldn't make the stories
we brought home any easier to tell.

IN HOUSTON

IN

HOUSTON

███████████ et al

v

HARRIS COUNTY TEXAS et al

JUDGES MOTIONS TO DISMISS

Bail ███ Plaintiffs seek to abolish

███ bail

███ to challenge

███ Texas ███

Plaintiffs allege   bail

is unconstitutional   because it fails

allege

the Eighth Amendment

ignore the

constitution

These claims should be dismissed

These challenges

should be dismissed

Plaintiffs seek to federalize

Harris County This is antithetical to our

past Plaintiffs   demand

the Court abandon

bail

███████████████████████████████████████

███████████████████████████████████████

██████████████████████

██

██

████████████████████████████████████ Plaintiffs

core complaint is ████████████ ████████████

████████████████████ is nothing ████████████

████████ resoundingly and repeatedly rejected ██████████

██

██

███████████████ Plaintiffs seek to invent ████████ █████████

███████████ the Fourteenth Amendment █████████████

██

██

██████████████████████████████████████

██

██

██ ████████████████████████████████████

████████ Plaintiffs equal protection claim fails █████████

██

██

██████████████████████████ bail █████████████████

████████████████████████████████████

███ been recognized ██████ since ████ the eighteenth century ████

███████████████████████████████████

█████████ bail █████████████████

████████████████ is and was constitutional

█████████████████████████

█████████████

███████████████████████████████

██████████████████████████ Plaintiff █████

lacks standing ██████ she is a fugitive ██████

██████████████████████ Plaintiff ██████ lacks

standing ██████ he was ██████ in jail ████████

█████████████████████████████

████████████████████████ Plaintiff █████ lacks

standing ██████

██████████████████████

Plaintiffs ████ alleges ████████████████████

████████████ Equal Protection ██████████████

███ Plaintiffs allege ██████████████████

████████████████ Plaintiffs claim ████

███████████████████████████

██

████████ Plaintiffs allege ██████████████████████

██████████████████████████████████ Plaintiffs allege

██

██

████████████ Plaintiffs   claim █████████████████████

██

██████████

████████████████████

██

Bail originated ████████████ 400 years ago ████████████████████

██

██

██

███

██

███

██████████

██

████████████████████████████████████ The issue ████████

████████ is not novel ████████ litigated since the beginning ████████████

██

bail is not unconstitutional

Plaintiffs propose a radical

jurisprudence

Under this view

the Fourteenth

Amendment would   overrule

the Eighth Amendment

The Fourteenth Amendment   the Eighth

Amendment

the Eighth Amendment

the Fourteenth Amendment

Pursuant to our federalist system the

defendants

must be

used as   an instrument of oppression

41

This system exists to █ prejudice

the

bail system

has proven █ an extremely effective tool

some criminal

defendants █ remain █ despite being able to bail out

the defendant █ their contacts

chosen not to post bond due to health

42

parent wants to stop drug use

or the defendant wishes to remain the

jail provides shelter multiple meals per day medical services

Plaintiffs claims

should be dismissed

Plaintiffs are asking Court to intervene

Plaintiffs' claims

should also be dismissed

Judges are not the creators of bail

the Judges

are immune from

damages

the Plaintiffs

claims should be dismissed

Plaintiffs' claims are really excessive

an effort   to avoid

the

text of the Eighth Amendment

Plaintiffs claims should be
dismissed Plaintiffs claims should be dismissed

Plaintiffs claims

should be dismissed

Plaintiffs claims have been
unanimously rejected

The specific claims

should be dismissed

Judges are immune

Plaintiffs' claims should be dismissed

the claims against

the Judges should be dismissed

NIGHT

In the night,—night asleep, her eyes, woman,
my woman, I name her as if she is mine,
as if these hours that pass for the night belong to us;

my nights belong to the memories I can't shake; my night
& this woman, my woman she tells me how it wasn't
supposed to be like this. This insight another Hail Mary,

another haymaker. We live somewhere between almost there
& not enough. Almost there. Her dreams & all that she lost
for me is a kind of accounting. My woman, not my woman,

not this night, not these nights: the mine is less mine more
hurt. More hover than anything else. Shadowcloud.
Or as she says it, you stalked me until I submitted. Love

shapes itself into my hands wrapped round her throat. Have you
loved like that? I'll call your PO is the thing she says,
on this night with the men I robbed still lingering, a threat

to the freedom I imagined she gave when we became
cliché: naked, tangled. This is always about me,
how violence called to me like my woman moans when she

thought all this was the promise of more than a funeral.
When I grabbed her like that the first time, her legs held me
tight. My woman thinking the cells in my past can make

. . .

her control this: all the ways I starve. She threatens
to call my history back as a constraint on madness.
She stared at me, once, & said she saw her brothers

doing life in my eyes. In this night, when we talk to each other,
it is in shouts. The quilt of solitary cells I've known confess
that my woman has never been my woman. How ownership

& want made me split that bastard's head into a scream
is what I'll never admit to her. What she
tells me: prison killed you my love, killed you so dead

that you're not here now, you're never here, you're always.
Her eyes closed at night & I awaken & swear she
stares at me, she is saying that brown liquor owns me, saying

that the cells own me & that there is no room for her, unless
she calls the police, the state, calls upon her pistol, & sets me free.

ESSAY ON REENTRY

Telling a story about innocence, won't conjure
acquittal. & after interrogation & handcuffs
& the promises of cops blessed with an arrest
before the first church service ended, I'd become
a felon. The tape recorder sparrowed
my song back to me, but guilt lacks a melody.
Listen, who hasn't waited for something
to happen? I know folks died waiting. I know
hurt is a wandering song. I was lost in my fear.
Strange how violence does that, makes the gun
vulnerable. I could not wait, & had no idea
what I was becoming. Later, in a letter, my
victim tells me: *I was robbed there; the food was great*
& drinks delicious, but I was robbed there. I would
consider going back. He said it as if I didn't know.
Why would he return to a memory like that?
As if there is a kind of bliss that rides shotgun
with the awfulness of a handgun & a dark night.
There is a Tupac song that begins with a life
sentence; imagine, I scribbled my name
on the confession, as if autographing a book.
Tell your mother that. Say the gun was a kiss
against the sleeping man's forehead,
say that you might have been his lover & that,
on a different night, he might have moaned.

ESSAY ON REENTRY

for Nicholas Dawidoff

Of prison, no one tells you the time
will steal your memories—until there's
nothing left but strip searches & the hole

& fights & hidden shanks & the spades games.

You come home & become a parade
of confessions that leave you drowning,
lost recounting the disappeared years.

You say fuck this world where background checks,
like your fingerprints, announce the crime.

Where so much of who you are betrays
guilt older than you: your pops, uncles,
a brother, two cousins, & enough
childhood friends for a game of throwback—

all learned absurdity from shackles.
But *we wear the mask that grins & lies.*
Why pretend these words don't seize our breath?
Prisoner, inmate, felon, convict.

Nothing can be denied. Not the gun
that delivered you to that place where

. . .

you witnessed the images that won't
let you go: Catfish learning to subtract,
his eyes a heroin-slurred mess;
Blue-Black doing backflips in state boots;
the D.C. kid that killed his cellmate.

Jesus. Barely older than you, he
had on one of the white undershirts
made by other men in prison, boxers, socks
that slouched, shackles gripping his shins.
Damn near naked. Life waiting.

Outside your cell, you could see them wheel
the dead man down the way. The pistol

you pressed against a stranger's temple
gave you that early morning. & now,
boxes checked have become your North Star,
fillip, catalyst to despair. Death
by prison stretch. Tell me. What name for
this thing that haunts, this thing we become.

ON VOTING FOR BARACK OBAMA IN A
NAT TURNER T-SHIRT

The ballot ain't never been a measure of forgiveness.
In prison, people don't even talk about voting,
about elections, not really, not the dudes
you remember, 'cause wasn't nobody Black
running no way. But your freedom hit just
in time to see this brother high-stepping with
the burden, with the albatross, willing
to confess that he knew people like you.
& you are free, you are what they call out
& off papers & living in a state where you're
not disenfranchised. In prison, you listened
to the ballot or the bullet & imagined that
neither was for you, having failed with
the pistol & expecting the ballot to be
denied. But nah, you found free & in line
notice that this is not like the first time
you & the woman you'd marry got naked
& sweated & moaned & funked up a room
not belonging to either of you. That lady
is with you now & a kid is in your arms,
& you are wearing a Nat Turner T-shirt
as if to make a statement at the family
reunion. Everyone around you is Black,
which is a thing you notice. & you know
your first ballot will be cast for a man
who has the swag that seems inherited.
It's early but there is no crust in your eyes.

You wanted this moment like freedom.
You cast a ballot for a Black man in
America while holding a Black baby.
Name a dream more American than
that, especially with your three felonies
serving as beacons to alert anybody
of your reckless ambition. That woman
beside you is the kind of thing fools
don't even dream about in prison &
she lets you hold your boy while voting,
as if the voting makes you & him
more free. Sometimes, it's just luck.
Just having moved to the right state
after the cell doors stop
clanking behind you. The son
in the arms of the man was mine,
& the arms of the man belonged
to me, & I wore that Nat Turner
T-shirt like a fucking flag, brown
against my brown skin.

EXILE

No letters distinguish my father's name
from my own. No signal for the mailman, the postman,
            my employer. The man before them is me
& not what happens after grief. We are no goldfinch,
instead a kind of crow, a murder of us looming.

                An employer searching our
history would find felonies & divorce proceedings, the online
account of our background a song of tragedy & regret.

A public defender or prosecutor seeking our truth
            finds a dozen men with portions of our names, variations &
fragments & records of men who've been called before

a judge for everything from domestic violence to traffic tickets
to something called jury trial prayer & everything I did
            that landed me in all those prison cells. There is no way
to distinguish us without a birth date, as if our first breath
            is a signature separating who from who. In 1960,

eight years before the King's assassination sparked the torching
of his city, my father was born; & twenty years later, just
as crack would make my father's home burn again, I arrived
            like that man's shadow. The room fills with us, when

I enter—our regrets our anchor, our history an echo that sounds
when I speak, the decade I now
                        own somehow more & more like the decades he has lost,
though, in a way, I know this is the kind of thing he'd call

. . .

        bullshit on & point out that there is nothing in the cracks
& tremors & baselines of my voice that suggest the sixth-story
window he leaped from as if to test the theory of man & flight
       & tattooed wings that I obsess over. & maybe he's right,

this unwieldy path of contrition or reform or mourning we
             both find ourselves walking has never been
wide enough. Still, I come from a man who's nursed
more than whisky, meaning who's nursed it all, from a pistol,

        to a prayer, to a small child in his arms that calls
him daddy. Those revelations are the kind of story a man
      who only has his own name could never own.

PARKING LOT

A confession begins when I walk into a parking lot.
Near empty, the darkness a kettle. The burner against
My skin cold like any story that ends this way.
The parking lot more of an opening than an opportunity.
The man was waiting for home, asleep in a car after
A working man's day. Everything I know of home
Is captured by the image of a man running from
The police, his arms flailing unlike any bird you'd expect
To fly. Walking into a parking lot begins a confession.
The burner is a key & afterwards there will be no home
To find. My boots echoed against the black of asphalt.
Hours before I flashed the burner on that family, I kissed
My kid goodnight. I told a woman that I loved her.
But when has love ever been enough.

PARKING LOT, TOO

A confession began when I walked out of that parking lot.
A confession began when I walked Black out of that parking lot.
A confession began when I, without combing my hair, dressed
For a day that would find me walking out of that parking lot.
There is so much to be said of a Black man with unkempt hair:
He meets the description of the suspect; suspect is running.
I ran away from things far less frightening than the police.
A confession began when I robed myself in black. A confession
Began when I walked out of that parking lot wearing a black
Hoodie. Things get exponentially worse when a hoodie is pulled
Over my unkempt air. A confession began when I walked out
Of that parking lot Black. A confession began when I walked
Out of that parking lot a Negro. A confession begins when
That nigga walked into the parking lot. A confession begins
When that nigga & the pistol he carries like a dick walked
Into that parking lot. A confession begins when everything you
See him doing is seen as sex. A confession begins when
That nigga walked into a parking lot & drove away with everything
Belonging to that white man. A confession begins when
My mother laid up with a man the complexion of that nigga's
Daddy. A confession begins when my mother births a child
In a city close enough to make me & that nigga almost related.
A confession begins when the police perceive us as one. We must
Be one. He could not have walked in & driven out & I walked
In & walked out on the same night & whatever gaps in the story
& slight differences in the features of our faces was just
More evidence that niggers will lie. A confession begins even if
I didn't have the fucking car. A confession begins, my confession
Began, with a woman stitching stars & stripes into a flag.

GOING BACK

after M.M.

If I return, it'll start with a pistol
& what happened
    last night, the dark a mask that
never hides
    enough. I'll pour the last of my
drink down so fast,
    I'll choke & cough & then
think about a half dozen
    Black boys sitting on crates in
what passed as woods
    around the way, just behind the
landscape of apartments
    where Slim told us he had
HIV. If I go back, I'll
    be thinking of him, & how he
shot the clerk in the
    7-Eleven during that robbery, killing
a man because
    he was dying. When Fat Boy
learned Slim had that shit,
    as we called it back then,
knowing no better than us,
                he wrapped
Slim up in a brother's
    embrace. It changed how I saw the
world. If I return,
    the past that I pretend defines me
will not explain the old

feeling of cuffs that capture
my hand's ambition. A sheriff's
car will take me down I-95, &
I'll tell myself the first time
I went down south was to go to
prison. All of my legacy
will be in my head, rattling
around in that four-door sedan
with the fucked-up suspension. I'll
ride through my memories,
will feel time constraining my
dreams. Returning will
take me through what'll feel like an
entire state filled with cities
named after prisons. My
birthdays of yesterday will
become the water that my head
struggles to break
through. & if I dared mourn &
say a prayer, but
nah, I wouldn't mourn or say any
prayers.

IN CALIFORNIA

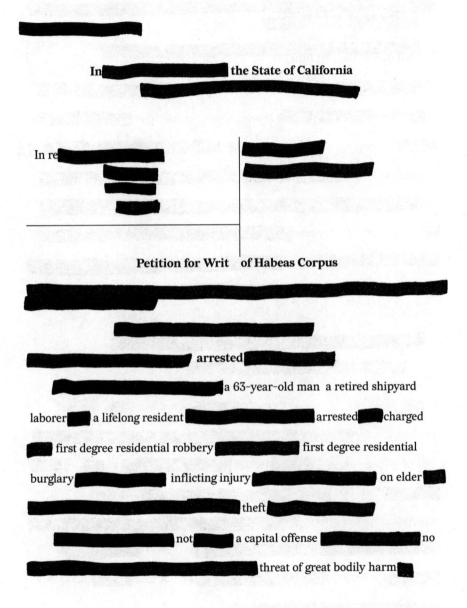

In ██████████████ the State of California

In re ████████████

Petition for Writ of Habeas Corpus

███████████ arrested ████████

███████████ a 63-year-old man a retired shipyard laborer ████ a lifelong resident ██████████ arrested ████ charged ████ first degree residential robbery ████████ first degree residential burglary ████████ inflicting injury ██████████ on elder ████ ████████ theft ████████ not ████ a capital offense ██████████ no ████████ threat of great bodily harm ██

██████████████████████████████████

████████████████

████████████████████████████

██████ defense requested release ██████

████████████████████ Humphrey's advanced age ████████

██████ lifelong resident of San Francisco ████████████

shipyard laborer ██████████████████████████

███████████████████████████████████████

██ lack of a recent criminal

███████████████████████████████████████

██████████████████████████

█████████████████████████████████

████████████████████████

██████ prosecutor requested $600,000 ██████ money bail ██ a criminal

protective order ███████████████████████████████

The judge denied ████████████ release ████████████████ set ██ bail ███

██████ $600,000 ████████████████████████ The court

emphasized public safety ████████████████████████████

███████████████████████████████ $600,000 ████████████

██████ Humphrey ████████████████ did not have ██████ money to

pay ████████████████

███████████████████████████████████

███████████████████████████████████

███████████████████████████████████

███████████████████

███████████████████████████████████

███████████████████████████████

██████████████████████████████ Humphrey argued

████████ bail ████ beyond his means ███ violated the Fourteenth

Amendment's ███████████████████████████████

████████████ the Eighth Amendment's ██████████████████

███████████████████████████████████

██████

████ prosecution argued ████████████████████

public safety ███ flight risk concerns █████████████ prosecutor

requested ███████████████████ detention ███ court denied

Humphrey's request █████████████████

███████████████████████████████████

███████████████████████████████████

███████████████████████████████████

███████████████████████████████████

██████

Humphrey presented ████ acceptance letter

Golden Gate for Seniors

asked to be released ████ to Golden Gate

emphasized ██ advanced age

treatment for ██ battle with addiction

too poor to pay the cash

petitioner asks ████ A writ of habeas corpus be issued

ordering ████ released

an expedited hearing

the court inquire into

ability to pay ████ release

not ████ to detain him ████ release

release

TEMPTATION OF THE ROPE

The link between us all
is tragedy, & these so many years
later, I am thinking of him,

all of twenty & gay &, maybe, more
free than any of us might ever be,
& this is one way of telling the story,

another one is aphorism, or threat:
blood on my knife or blood on my dick;
which is to confess: surviving that young &

beautiful & willing to walk every day
as if wearing sequins meant believing, always,
there is a thing worth risking doom.

There is no reason for me to think of him
now, especially with the football player's
hanging body eclipsing another prison

cell, except, maybe the kid whose name
I can't remember but walk I can, had mastered
something the dead man's singing legs could

never, how not to abandon the body's
weight, & how to make the body expand,
to balloon, to keep becoming, until even

.   .   .

the danger could not swallow you.
One day I watched him, full of fear for
my own fragility & wondered how he dared

own so much of himself, openly. For all
I know every minute in those cells
was safe for the kid whose name

I cannot recall. But how can a man ever
be safe like that, when you are so
beautiful the straight ones believe it &

want to talk to you as if they love you
& want you to dare them to believe
that some things in this world must be

too lovely to ever be broken.

BALLAD OF THE GROUNDHOG

—where cities get lost to time,
everyone knows the groundhog's story,
      a wild animal caged, a climb cleaved,
the beast transformed into something gory,

a caution or a flag or just inevitable.
      They say he almost flew, catapulted
before the rest happened. Anviled
by the metal fence, cast as freedom's insult

in this county where states still turn
      men into numbers. There's no city
where I can feel free. Time is fucking
      inconsolable is what I mean, a starved sea

& sometimes there is nothing—just
days & their ruthless abundance.
      By the time I heard the woodchuck's
tale, I'd been returning to prison as penance,

      circling black holes that turn the barren
lands dense: avenues & alleyways
      buried inside sadness of castaways
lost to the clink. Who prays

for the groundhog? The Cut
is a landscape of cells dug into red dirt—
      Who with a state number outruns
the fate of red dirt? The rodent's hurt?

. . .

I owe my ears a debt for this burden.
  The groundhog believed in
escaping the steel bars around him.
  Home was gleaming metal, the linchpin

of shackles & handcuffs. Who
   wants to awaken to that spring?
When I ask my cousin, who knows
more prisons than cities, he's calling

  the Cut a fucking deathtrap, as if
he knew the beast. The groundhog
  a legend & caution. & Janis Joplin might
have been right, but for the epilogue:

the marmot, small-eared rodent, lost
  everything; eclipsed, like all wild
things aching for release. The fence
  tempted; one afternoon it exiled

the wobbling-near-leaping thing
  with saw-teeth sure to haunt.
A groundhog, rabid animal, any human
entangled in razor wire, wants

  to be more. We all, when held
that way, will struggle, twist the blades'
edges deeper. & so shanked
  on a spiraling cosmos, the serenade

. . .

of the grass rat became a story
        we all know. When the fence's tines
grab hold, they will embrace like prison
strangles anyone doing time—

& this is true, whatever the
        groundhog's fate. Maybe men ain't
as wild as we think. & no one
came to cut the whistle-pig free.

NOVEMBER 5, 1980

I have called, in my wasted youth, the concrete slabs
Of prison home. Awakened to guards keeping tabs
On my breath. Bartered with every kind of madness,
The state's mandatory minimums & my own callus.
I've never called a man father; & while sleep, twice
Wrecked cars; drank whisky straight; nothing suffices—
I fell in love with sons I wouldn't give my name. Once
Swam at midnight in the Atlantic's violence,
Under the water, rattling broke the silence. I cussed
Men with fists like hambones & got beaten to dust.
Buried memories in my gut that would fill a book.
I've carried pistols but have never held a bullet.
There is frightful little left for me to hold in fear,
Definitely not the debt that threatens to hollow
Me. I've abhorred transparency, confessed to so-and-so,
But what of it matters, in this life so much has troubled,
& the few things that didn't, never failed to baffle.

& EVEN WHEN THERE IS SOMETHING TO COMPLAIN ABOUT

There are those who fuck,
whose bodies collapse into yearning.
This is in the middle of all anger,
the sweat glistening, the moans
become something primal. The first
time I felt like I owned something,
she was moaning in my ear
as if I was more animal than man.
Caught in the precipice. She says,
fuck me like we just met. & she means,
like all of the shit that is ruining everything
hasn't happened, she means when we
thought how we joined together
augured some mythic kind of joy.
& yes, this is the fantasy, wanting
to be wanted. She called me hers
as if the state didn't already have claim
to most of me. So sincere, that kind
of want, when talk verges on orgasm.
But I was uncomfortable with my own
hunger, & how it cascaded into
this thing that left me empty & her wanting.

MURAL FOR THE HEART

Tonight is not for my woman, who would touch me
before we speak; not when the accumulation
of our yesterdays hang like the last dusk before us—
each memory another haunting thing. Not when buried
somewhere behind us is all that the past, that we,
will not let die, history our prophecy & albatross, the myth
we measure the marrow. Every story worth telling
has a thousand beginnings. Let me tell you this one:
There was this one night on a road trip. She, my wife, was not
there. Already rehearsing my absence, practicing the dance
of raising boys alone. Distance our disaster. & so, if I say
the trouble began when the car stalled, I would be lying. But
the car did stall, every light inside flashed as if
the emergency was something breaking inside of she & I,
& not just an empty tank. Everyone wants a chance
to be a hero, & so, when I climbed out the truck's front seat,
already I had measured the distance from the truck to the station.
A thousand feet. I once lifted my woman & carried her
on my back from where we stood to the bed that I would turn
into what remains when lies become shrapnel. Have you seen
a man push his body against a thing as if love alone
would move it? That night there were three of us riding. My
woman was not there. Two of us climbed out, rolled up sleeves,
began pushing. Muscles strained against the darkness, the heft
of the truck lurching, at best. When the scrawny kid joined,
his body lost inside his coat, we thought ourselves blessed.
A tampon run, he said, explaining why he was there, on this
street so late at night, his girlfriend on the side of the road

& my woman five hundred miles away, as if to say
part of love is pretending to be a hero for strangers. The truck
barely moved, the way love barely moves, when weighed
down by memories. Before long there were four of us pushing,
the thousand feet still a thousand feet. & then
we stopped, which is to say we realized: the thing you want
can break you. We all knew that in time our legs would shake,
that our bodies would betray us & admit that the heart,
though not useless, lacks the thing needed for some miracles.
& yet, against this truth, I keep praying my woman,
who is no more mine than any woman can belong to a man,
but is her own, constellation of music & desire, as is anyone,
will forgive history, knowing a thousand angels stand beside,
exhausted, too, though certain the heft of their wings will bring
a gale fierce enough to lift this hurt that we refuse to name.

ESSAY ON REENTRY

for Fats, Juvie & Star

       Fats ain't never killed nobody,
but has known more years in cells than cities,
than school, than lovers, than his favorite
cousin lived, more years than freedom.

     We met before M- ran his time up
over a 5-inch black & white, before K- broke
somebody's jaw with the lock in the sock.
Back when everyone thought they'd go home;
before T- went home & was murdered; before
J- went home & came back. He gives me

the math on men I did my bid with: *yesterday I sat*
at a table with Star, remember him? I was looking
at his balding head & he was looking at the grays
that cover my crown. I looked at Juvie at a near
table both crown & beard stubble completely gray. . . .

     We first discovered jail cells decades ago,
as teenagers & just today, a mirror reminded
me of my disappeared self; androgenic alopecia:
a word for our vanishing hair. Latin describing
how time will cause everything to recede.
No word exists for the years that we've lost

   ·   **·**   **·**

to prison. & I thought, Fats, describing a moment
he'd shared with men he's known for decades,
was thinking about all that lost. But, he writes,
looking at the landscape of gray that had become
them, he realized it was *far from over,*

    because, all these rounds later, prison ain't
still undefeated, & one of these days we
might find us some free.

CONFESSION

If I told her how often I thought
Of prison she would walk out
Of the door that's led just as much
To madness as any home we
Desired, she would walk out & never
Return; my employers would call
Me a liar & fire me. My dreams are
Not all nightmares, but this history
Has turned my mind's landscape into
A gadroon. I do not sing. Have lied
For so many months now that truth
Harbingers lost. Sleeping beside her
When a memory is holding me tight
As she did before the lies turned
Everything into a battle, I once
Gasped & lurched & tried to
Strangle the pillow she'd placed
Beneath my head. Imagining me
Explaining that to her, while still
Shivering like a panicked & broken
Man. I stopped believing in G-d
Long before then, but that night,
When outside there was no light
But darkness, I swore something
Of what inevitable is touched me.
My children slept with their light on.
I walked to their still-lit room. My
Son was asleep & his brother draped

Over his body as if he were the
Pillow. The way he loved his brother
Was everything my time in a cell denied
Me. If I told my woman that, she
Would want to know if I thought
I deserved all that lost. Her mother
Wonders why I won't let it go & hold
On to the happiness in this life we
Have. But how do I explain that outside
On nights like this, is where I first
Learned just how violent I might be?
That, I think of prison because in all
These years I still can't pronounce
The name of my victim.

IN MISSOURI

IN ████ MISSOURI

████ et al

v

THE CITY OF FERGUSON

The Plaintiffs ████ people ████ jailed by
the City ████████████
████ the City kept a human
████ in its jail ████ the person
████ pleaded ████ poverty ████
████ held ████ indefinitely
████ threatened abused
████ left to languish ████ frightened
family members could ████ buy their freedom ████
████

impoverished cannot

endure grotesque treatment overcrowded cells

denied toothbrushes toothpaste soap subjected to the stench

of excrement and refuse surrounded by walls smeared

with mucus and blood for days and weeks

bodies

cover the entire cell floor

untreated illnesses infections in open wounds

days weeks

filthy bodies huddle in cold a single thin

blanket

they lose

weight they suffer

they must listen

to the screams they sit

without natural light

when they will be allowed to leave

These physical abuses

Jail guards   taunt   people

jail guards

laugh   humiliate them

shivering women   forced to

share blankets   officers shout   stanky ass

dykes   dirty whores

City officials   employees

built a   scheme

designed to brutalize   to punish   to profit   The architect

the City of Ferguson

The City of Ferguson

the rest of the Saint Louis

modern debtors prison

the City of Ferguson

devastated the City's poor   trapping them   in

debts extortion and cruel jailings

The treatment

reveals systemic illegality

The City has

a

a

Dickensian system that   violates the

most vulnerable

the City of Ferguson

the

City's conduct is unlawful

It   has been the policy   to jail

people

the ████ practice ████ to jail indigent ████

the ████ practice ████ to hold prisoners

indefinitely

the ████ practice ████ to issue

invalid ██ warrants to threaten

to hold arrestees in jail

arbitrarily

to confine

people in grotesque dangerous and

inhumane conditions a Kafkaesque journey

a lawless and labyrinthine scheme of

perpetual debt

HOUSE OF UNENDING

1.

The sinner's bouquet, house of shredded & torn
    Dear John letters, upended grave of names, moon
        Black kiss of a pistol's flat side, time blueborn
& threaded into a curse, Lazarus of hustlers, the picayune
Spinning into beatdowns; breath of a thief stilled
        By fluorescent lights, a system of 40 blocks,
        Empty vials, a hand full of purple cranesbills;
Memories of crates suspended from stairs, tied in knots
Around street lamps; the house of unending push-ups,
        Wheelbarrows & walking 20s; the daughters
        Chasing their fathers' shadows, sons that upset
The wind with their secrets, the paraphrase of fractured,
        Scarred wings flying through smoke; each wild hour
        Of lockdown, hunger time & the blackened flower.

2.

Of lockdown, hunger time & the blackened flower—
    Ain't nothing worth knowing. Prison becomes home;
The cell: a catacomb that cages & the metronome
    Tracking the years that eclipse you. History authors

Your death, throws you into that din of lost hours.
    Your mother blames it all on your X chromosome,
Blames it on something in the blood, a Styrofoam
Cup filled with whisky leading you to court disfavor,

. . .

To become drunk on count-time & chow-call logic.
    There is no name for this thing that you've become:
Convict, prisoner, inmate, lifer, yardbird, all fail.
    If you can't be free, be a mystery. An amnesic.
Anything. But avoid succumbing to the humdrum:
Swallowing a bullet or even just choosing to inhale.

3.

Swallowing a bullet or even just choosing to inhale,
    Both mark you: pistol or the blunt to the head
Escorting you through the night. Your Yale—
    An omen, the memories, the depression, the dead

& how things keep getting in the way of things.
When he asked you for the pistol, & you said no,
    The reluctance wasn't about what violence brings.
His weeping in your ear made you regret what you owed.

On some days, the hard ones, you curse the phone,
    The people calling collect, reaching out, all buried,
Surrounded by bricks. On some days, you've known
You wouldn't answer, the blinking numbers as varied

As the names of the prisons holding on to those lives,
Holding on, ensuring that nothing survives.

4.

    Holding on, ensuring that nothing survives,
Not even regret. That's the thing that gets you,
Holding on to memories like they're your archives,
    Like they're there to tell you something true

About what happened. My past put a skew
    On how I held her. Unaccustomed to touch,
I knew only dream & fantasy. Try to see through
That mire & find intimacy. It was just so much.

    & then, the yesterdays just become yesterday,
A story that you tell yourself about not dying,
Another thing, when it's mentioned, to downplay.
That's what me & that woman did, trying

To love each other. What kind of fool am I,
Lost in what's gone, reinventing myself with lies.

5.

Lost in what's gone, reinventing myself with lies:
I walk these streets, ruined by what I'd hide.
Jesus died for somebody's sins, but not mine.

I barely see my daughters at all these days.
    Out here caught up, lost in an old cliché.
But tell me, what won't these felonies betray.

Did a stretch in prison to be released to a cell.
    Returned to a freedom penned by Orwell.
My noon temptation is now the Metro's third rail.

In my wallet, I carry around my daguerrotype,
    A mugshot, no smiles, my name a tithe.
What must I pay for being this stereotype?

. . .

The pistols I carried into the night, my anchor;
The crimes that unraveled me, my banner.

6.

The crimes that unraveled me, my banner.
    Only a fool confesses to owning that fact.
Honesty a sinkhole; the truth doomed to subtract
Everything but prayer, turn my breath into failure.

    Whisky after prison made me crave amber,
Brown washing my glass until I'm smacked.
    The murder of crows on my arm an artifact
        Of freedom: what outlasts even the jailor.

    Alas, there is no baptism for me tonight.
No water to drown all these memories.
    The rooms in my head keep secrets that indict
Me still; my chorus of unspoken larcenies.
    You carry that knowledge into your twilight,
& live without regret for your guilty pleas.

7.

& live without regret for your guilty pleas—
    Shit. Mornings I rise twice: once for a count
That will not come & later with the city's
    Wild birds, who find freedom without counsel.

    I left prison with *debts no honest man could pay.*
Walked out imagining I'd lapped my troubles,
    But a girl once said no to my unlistening ears, dismayed
    That I didn't pause. Remorse can't calm those evils.

. . .

I've lost myself in some kind of algebra
That turns my life into an equation that zeroes
 Out, regardless of my efforts. Algophobia
Means to fear pain. I still fear who knows

All I've done. Why regret this thing I've worn?
The sinner's bouquet; house, shredded & torn.

ACKNOWLEDGMENTS

These lists get longer the older you are, and I'm tempted to just say for all of y'all. But there are people that have to be named.

Thanks to the people who gave me fellowships that allowed me to work on this book: the Guggenheim Foundation, National Endowment of Arts, New America Foundation, Emerson Foundation. But also, to some specific fellowships developed and created to support work challenging our incarceration practices. I'm thinking about Agnes Gund and the Arts for Justice Fund. I still remember when Elizabeth Alexander had me come to the meeting where Aggie, Kat, Helena Huang, and Tanya Coke were all sitting around this table as I talked about what would become the Redaction Project, a portfolio of prints that I made with Titus Kaphar. So, thank y'all, there is a particular kind of vision needed to know that art can be influential and lead to change without being didactic. Thanks to Titus Kaphar. We turned some conversations about art and fatherhood into something wild and lyrical. Also, can't forget the SOZE's Right of Return. Or PEN's Writing for Justice Fellowship. These fellowships weren't ever really about the money, but about creating a community across discipline and conversation. And many thanks to Jonathan Plutzik, Deborah Plutzik-Briggs, and the entire Betsy Hotel family. I've written parts of two books spending time with you and hope the writing does some justice to Hyam Plutzik's memory and legacy.

And then, it's always returning to my people. John Murillo, Randall Horton, and Marcus Jackson. (When the Symphony going back on tour?) Tyehimba Jess, who got secret stories of my NASCAR driving skills. Afaa Weaver, my old head. Marie Howe, who is always out there to listen to me. Rachel Eliza Griffiths, Nicole Sealey, Jericho Brown, Safiya Sinclair, Mitchell Jackson, and everyone else who came through and performed during the MoMA show. Part of all of that was me saying, y'all writing the work that pushes me. To Kiese Laymon, who heard a bunch of these joints when they were handwritten. Dude, the work you're doing pushes and inspires me. To Mitchell Jackson—between, me, you, and Kiese we got a mean three-on-three squad. And messing around with Kathryn Belden, who also deserves a shout out here for digging the prose and the poetry, we might cause some real new memory in this art thing. I'm missing folks. Willie Perdomo, Greg Pardlo, A Van Jordan, and the rest of the Stairwell Crew. Brian Gilmore, Ernesto Mercer, DJ Renegade, and Toni Lightfoot. To Yao Glover. Man we go back farther than most of the folks I might name in a list like that, and the thing about it that matters is after I told you I'd served time in prison, you asked me if I wrote, if I was a poet. Ain't much realer than that. To Asha French, 'cause sometimes your siblings don't share your parents. And to Lori Gruen, who's lived with these poems and my ramblings for quite some time now. I write these acknowledgments like this book might be my last. 'Cause you never know.

To my dad, looking back, so many of these poems seem to be me saying something to you. May we figure out what that is before it's all over.

And of course, this gets written because Marcus, Tony, Cee, we all lived way too many of these stories. But we came through. And that right there is damn near enough.

And to the immediate fam. Moms, all these poems exist 'cause you had me reading and thinking thinking mattered. Aunt Violet, you know, four-leaf clovers are the signature of my life and I owe you. And that me and your youngest son gave too much of our lives to prison, we owe you and my moms for that. May we repay that debt. I can name everyone. Grandma, Tricia, Darren, Tom, Pandora. Kim. Brian. Delonte. Nikki. Marquita. Pebbles. Aja. Josh. Mack. Zakiya. Jay. Who am I forgetting? Blame it on this deadline. Yes, we don't always talk, but whatever these things are that I do with words started with trying to get a word in around y'all. And even in the silence I love y'all.

And to Terese, Micah, and Miles. There is never enough of the joy and love and hope that you add onto my life in the poems I write, but I wouldn't be able to write them if that joy wasn't there.

Finally. For Markeese Turnage, Christopher Tunstall, Terrell Kelly, Rojai Fentress, Kevin Williams, and Anthony Winn. I know y'all by names like Keese and Juvie and Star and Fats and Luke and Absolut. And since first publishing this book, Fats and Juvie and Luke have all found freedom. Keese and Star, y'all day is on the horizon. I could say a lot, but I'm a say what Fats has taken to saying to me: thanks for the soup. I could have been a whole lot of things in this world but it was y'all and a rack of other dudes I only remember in dreams or when y'all remind me of them that first believed some of this was possible. All of the living that's happening in those prison cells, all the desperation and the fight, these poems are born out of that. And may we all find us some freedom soon.

NOTES

On the Redaction Poems

Civil Rights Corps (https://www.civilrightscorps.org/) is a nonprofit organization dedicated to challenging systemic injustice in the American legal system. One of its central areas of advocacy and litigation has been the money bail system. Every night, there are 450,000 human beings awaiting trial in U.S. jail cells solely because they cannot make a payment. CRC challenges wealth-based detention and promotes anti-carceral alternatives to human caging that are less restrictive, more effective, and grounded in holistic community engagement and empowerment. Their work has freed tens of thousands of people from jail cells, helped to elevate the issue of money bail into the popular consciousness, and is setting a precedent that will forever change the bail-setting process in the United States.

Four poems in this collection, "In Alabama," "In Houston," "In California," and "In Missouri" were redacted from legal documents that CRC filed to challenge the incarceration of people because they could not afford to pay bail. These poems use redaction, not as a tool to obfuscate, but as a technique that reveals the tragedy, drama, and injustice of a system that makes people simply a reflection of their bank accounts.

On the Type

The title pages, page numbers, and redacted poems are typeset in Redaction, a new font commissioned for the Redaction Project, a series of prints created by Dwayne in collaboration with the visual artist Titus Kaphar. Created by Forest Young and Jeremy Mickel, the Redaction font borrows from and transforms classic legal fonts into a statement about redaction and the role of the literal and figurative imagery of fonts to make meaning.

Publication Acknowledgments

Thanks to the many magazines and anthologies that have published versions of these poems: *Poetry, Tin House, Kenyon Review, Iron Horse Literary Review*, the Marshall Project, and the anthology *America, We Call Your Name*.

I've always thought of my own writing as having something of the desire of the quiltmaker. A book, filled with thousands of words, will sometimes have a few moments—echoes of the work of others, homages to poems and poets that gave me voice and belief. Or, as my friend Patrick Rosal describes it, "this is a very Filipino practice of embedding something borrowed . . . grafted into what you are making as a way of praise, prayer, singing . . . [i]t's all prayer to me, by which I mean a kind of devotion, discovery through attention." I always recast the line, present it in a way that makes of it something new, situated in a way that adds layers to the experience. Figuratively, it's called an allusion; where I'm from, it's just called a shout-out; the aim is for it to be recognized immediately, like seeing an old friend. *When I say a Big verse I'm only bigging up my brother.* This book is no different. And it is all prayer, the kind that sustained me when I had no name for g-d.

Like anyone else, I knew Springsteen—but, unlike most, I'd never heard his music. Then, I got lost in it. Earworm. Hours and hours for months of *Nebraska* and the rest. In "House of Unending" I slip in a line from "Atlantic City" and "Johnny 99." In both songs, the speaker refers to how empty pockets lead to crime and disaster: "I had debts no honest man could pay." I spin the line back on itself, using it to speak to a man that left prison with debts that stem from memories of crime and violence and regret.

The first line of Patti Smith's "Gloria" is "Jesus died for somebody's sins but not mine." The song is a cover of Them's "Gloria." But not a cover, because more than half of the words of Smith's "Gloria" are her own, creating a conversation between Them's and her work. It's all funky. And for me, Smith's riffing on a rejection of the religion, becomes, like my take on Springsteen's line, obsessing over regret and responsibility. *Jesus died for somebody's sins but not mine, mine I suffer for.* This is what the speaker of "House of Unending" admits.

I read Rita Dove's poem "Canary" while doing time at a dangerous and wild prison in Virginia where prisoners were confined in a cell for twenty-three hours each day. I was barely eighteen years old then. Had never heard "Strange Fruit." Never heard of Billie Holiday. The poem's final line, "If you can't be free, be a mystery," stayed with me for an entire prison sentence, becoming one of the things I carried. Two decades later, I still carried the line in my head. And it shows up here, in the second sonnet of "House of Unending," a nod to surviving while staving off invisibility. And a reminder for me of how a single line in a poem can be a gesture to the reader's survival. And, finally, as a kind of admission to myself: it's a miracle to know part of who I became was because of a line in a poem.

And yet, despite it all, "we were the mask that grins in lies," as I write in "Essay on Reentry," alluding to Paul Laurence Dunbar's "We Wear the Mask." I think Dunbar is the poet that made Du Bois's veil make sense for me—which is to say, Du Bois, in my mind, has always alluded to Dunbar.

Those who know will hear these lines and think immediately of Dove's "Canary," of Springsteen's "Atlantic City," of Dunbar's "We Wear the Mask," of Smith's "Gloria." Those who don't will read these notes and return to that work, and hopefully they'll carry the lines around in their heads as I have.